MW01491340

George Howell

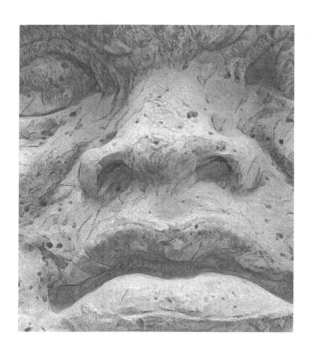

Cholla Needles Arts & Literary Library
a non-profit organization
Joshua Tree, CA

## Acknowledgments

"The Empty House," "The Mountain/Ahab in the Desert," "The Leonardo Mountains," "Pájaros Callados/Quiet Birds" and "Cul de Sac" appeared in Cholla Needles #5. "The Leonardo Mountains" also appeared in Cholla Needles 2017 Yearbook. "Scorpion," "Contrails" and "Headlights on the Rolling Hills" appeared in Mojave River Review, Spring 2017. "The Nest," "Guns & Fire," "Smoke Tree," "Earthquake," "If you find Buddha, shoot him" and "Keys" appeared in Cholla Needles, Issue #16. "Petals," "The Olympics of My Errors," "Fireball over Wonder Valley" and "Sex and Death in the Hi-Desert" were included in Cholla Needles #25.

All photographs belong to George Howell, except the author photo, taken by M.T. Evans.

https://www.chollaneedles.com

After a rough week in Menifee,
watching my uncle sliding towards death,
I've needed to feel the stony embrace
of the mountains in our valley.

*--from an unfinished poem*

*This book is dedicated to my wife, Mary Best, who always encourages me, and to my brother Mark, who didn't get to see this.*

California &
Life in the Desert

## Sex & Death in the Hi-Desert

The big female snout beetle plays dead
when I prod her with a stick,
Apoininae-like
as the field guide says,
her smaller mate lying dead
in the debris collected
in the plastic water bottle,
his legs and snout curled
in the rigid repose of death.

Life is fragile here
in the Hi-Desert
& even the best of intentions
can lead to regrets.

I found them fucking
in the dirty bird feeder
my wife cut out of a water jug,
photographed them
& then anchored the bottle
to a creosote bush
for protection.
They couldn't crawl up
the slippery plastic sides
& the small male died.

In the snapshot,
he is pressed up against
her fertile roundness
just as I might lay against my wife's hips,
content & ready for sleep.

Even the best of intentions
can lead to regrets.

I lowered the plastic feeder
& got some coffee.
When I returned,
the big female was gone.

8/27/14

## Martin Mull

What color is California?
Green and bronze,
succulent orange
and purple,
the sensuous dream
of arroyos stolen
and film developing.

Martin Mull
is monochrome,
the black and white
dream below
the dream.

The day dream
of these paintings
follows a broken outline—
The walls of the ranch house
left incomplete,
the lawn mower frozen
over the half-tundra
of a front yard,
Dad in his flannel shirt,
Mom in her apron—
The dream of the '50s
bleached and left out
to dry like the monochrome
of a sleeping child's dream,

the busy distracted
mental life
we never know
except in the surrender
of the Other
to love or hate.

California waking
to the negative
half-life of its
disappointments,
a collection
of private snapshots
recovered from the attic
of a dream.

11/18/10

George Howell

## The Shit Index

The small cat
twitches her tail
as she sticks her face
into the pile of scat,
old shit left over
from the last time
a coyote
trailed our fence
and relieved itself
before drifting back
into the shadows
of the creosote bushes.

Every morning,
I walk our cat
around the house,
watching out for her
while I check for new poop,
the shit index
that registers
the level of risk
in our backyard.

We lost her two sisters
last year to cancer
and a random coyote.
I don't want to lose her,
as well, to carelessness
or lack of attention.

We stay vigilant.

I protect her
as I try to protect myself
from the fears that
pass through
my dreams
like the shadow
of a coyote
in the moonlight,
moving deliberately
along the length
of our fence.

2/9/15

## *The Empty House*

Off to the side of the road,
a deserted house
　　　looking onto the long plain
　　　of shrubs and gravel—
　　　　　　A house with its share
　　　　　　of ghosts?

I want to fill
the empty house
　　　with my emptiness,
I want to sit
in the ruined living room
　　　and look out at the snow
　　　on San Gorgonio,
　　　at the clouds marching
　　　across the sky,
　　　at the peach sunset.

Watch what is full and outside
　　　of the walls of this empty house.

I am an empty house,
standing upright
and facing the fullness
　　　of the outside
　　　with eyes emptied of
　　　opinion, expectation
　　　or hope.

An empty house.

5/10/15

## Trapped Bird

The pretty green bird
flies over the doorway,
a reluctant guest,
and panicking,
bangs against the window,
frantic wings caught behind
the caramel reed blinds.

We lift the blinds to free it,
but the bird flies higher up the window—
Frantic flutter panic.

I tip one side of the blinds
against the window,
to make a wall,
tip the other side open,
and the bird falls free.

Suspended, its beak open,
the profoundly deep black well
of its fear inexpressible,
eyes fierce, and
then it is gone.

We were talking about our fears,
of aging and change
and our human weaknesses,
and the bird's dark throat
swallows them up
and we are free.

5/14/13

## Rescuing Insects

It's a small mitzvah,
dropping the plastic hummus container
down around a spider
or a small moth
caught in the window screen.

Slip a piece of paper
under the lip
and carry the poor bug
outside.

Swimming in Suzanne's pool,
watching dust devils swirl about
on the desert floor
in front of the blue mountains
and bees and tiny flies
and wasps
flounder and drown
in the blue chlorinated water.

Cup you hands
and scoop up the yellow jacket.
It stands on your fingers,
buzzing wetness off its transparent wings
and flies away.

A little act of kindness
for small, overlooked
beings.

5/14/13

## Roadrunner

I know,
we shouldn't feed
the roadrunner.
But we have
pumpkin seeds
and raisins
and he is so
personable,
trotting from
the aviary
where the zebra-striped
finches from New Zealand
squeal and peep
in the morning sunlight.

He trots towards me,
one foot ahead of the other,
a succession of feet
like frames in a stop motion picture,
sneaking stealthfully
away from the bird cage
where a dead baby finch
hangs by its dried foot
from the only nest
it ever knew.

5/15/13

## *Scorpion*

I don't like to kill things.

The critters live here, we're just visitors.
Remembering the sidewinder
that crawled under my chair
in the garage last year,
sunlight sparkling on the silvery arms
of the lawn chair & the snake
finally slid away as the sun went down.

I don't like to kill things.

I found a scorpion sitting on the air mattress
where Maria slept last night.
I'm cleaning up her bedding & there he is,
all bristly, pincers at the ready.
I try to sweep him out the door
with a broom
& he scoots underneath the baseboard,
tail curled up like an angry fist.

What do you do?

Live by chance? Leave the door open
& hope he exits gracefully?

What if he scurries into the other room,
burrows into our suitcases,
or crawls into the pile of sheets
laying on the other bed?

Snip off his tail?
That's where the poison is,
& leave him defenseless
against his enemies?

What do you do?

You get a sharp knife from the kitchen drawer
& jab it precisely under the baseboard—
A puddle of blood staining the Saltillo tiles.

I hate to kill things.
Sometimes you don't have a choice.

11/6/12

## Guns & Fire

I strike a match to light my cook stove,
a friendly fire to warm the leftovers.

I could hold the match up to my lips
& blow it out with my breath,
or I could hold it out
to the Santa Anas
& set my valley on fire.

Smoke rises from the other side
of the mountains—
The Marines shooting off big guns,
or a crashed helicopter burning,
or the neighborhood crater
waking up in Amboy?

Where there is smoke,
there is a question mark.

Guns & fire,
what a nightmare.

Whole neighborhoods are burning
in Los Angeles
& the winds will be more vicious tonight.

& somewhere outside of a post office,
or a little wooden church,
someone is waiting—
If he doesn't cradle an AR-15,
he'll hold a box of matches.

12/06/17

## The Mountain/Ahab in the Desert
*For David Landrey*

The hump of the mountain emerges
out of the clouds
and recedes back into the clouds,
the layer of snow on its flank
as white as spume.

Like an adversary waiting on the horizon.

An exile, I am miles from the ocean.

Does the wind cast away the waves
the way it tosses gravel
across the windshield?
Does the wind make it impossible
to stand on the good leg
and the wooden one?

Nature signifies its disapproval
and we draw our lines in the sand.

Is it unjust, or simply absurd, to take it to task
for the misfortunes that sweep us off
the good foot and the other one?

No matter how quickly I drive,
the mountain recedes into the distance
like an adversary slipping beyond the horizon.

Its lack of humility
weighs on my soul.

5/18/15

## *Cement Bag*

The eye has a habit
of picking at things,
picking at the dust this gusty wind
pitches into my eyes,
picking out the plastic cement bag
which laid in the dusty road
where I saw it everyday
as I walked to the mailbox—
The wind picked it up like a kite
and cast it against a distant
creosote bush, where it flaps
like a national flag
my mind can't quite recognize.

Is it true my mind can't touch
the mental objects my eye picks up,
can't carry it like a bag of coffee
you bring to a friend?

What a shame!

No matter how far I stretch my arm,
I'll never touch the mountains out there,
shrouded in dust on this windy day.

But I can still look,
and in the act of looking,
find words as light
as a cast away
cement bag.

1/31/14

## Smoke Tree
### For Jeni Bate

Our eyes align
along the horizon,
prisoners of our feet,
firmly anchored to the earth.

And the sky is a sigh
of promise and release,
the free range of cloud
and soul.

You cut the skyscape
into a stack of cards,
and rearranged the clouds
like the ascending branches
of a tree.

The smoke tree,
child of the earth
and the sky.

Our two feet firmly planted
before the canvas,
we follow the plumes of smoke
into the blue air,
yearning for
freedom.

1/6/18

## *The Olympics of My Errors*

If I make it to the end
  of the giant slalom of this poem,
I'll smash my helmet against the snow
  and cry,
        overwhelmed by the exhilaration
        of my mistakes.

The critics locked inside my helmet
chide with the authority
of television commentators—
    "That mistake will damage his reputation."
    "Not enough wax on his words."
    "If he just put a little more spin
        on that double entendre."

At the end of the slope of this poem,
my fellow poets and competitors
    huddle like tiny figures on a game board,
    welcoming each other as they crash
    at the finish line—
        "What a great mistake!"
        "That disaster was breathtaking!"
        "Wow, I've never fallen on *my* face
          with that much grace!"

They slap each other's backs,
rubbing big gloved hands across
    shiny helmets,
      the camaraderie of losers
        who know the visceral joy
        of failure.

Aloft, spinning in free fall,
  all of my bad word choices,
    feeble sentences,
      self-indulgent emotions,
        romantic sorrows,
          really dumb ideas,
shake inside my helmet
like seeds in a hollow maraca.

I don't care.
The critical earth,
    with all of its pine trees
    and ski trails leading nowhere
      can stay pinned
      to the wall of its certainty
        like a calendar
        for the year that never comes.

I'm in the air.
I'm flying.
I'm never coming down.

2/17/18

## *Fireball over Wonder Valley*

Yes, a fireball will certainly get my attention—
       Fireworks on a non-holiday,
       a jellyfish bursting,
       gassy tendrils
       dropping from the sky,
       burning.

I put down my fork
& pick up the phone.

A cross street, the operator asks.

My binoculars & I
can't spot a street sign
in the dusk on Humbug Mountain.

By the time the flashing red
emergency vehicle slow climbs the hillside
& heads east, the embers to the southwest
are out for the night.

I can spot a fireball in the dusk,
but I just can't see the mythology
of Wonder Valley.

The outsiders call our valley
a vortex of mysticism,
a hideaway for ashram hucksters,
a frontier outpost for Buddha.

This was no spiritual exercise.

Some folks blew up a car
& left the bushes burning.
Bomb & run. No Austin.
They didn't rocket into the sky
with the jellyfish.

Do I see the getaway car—
Headlights weaving through the dusk,
but eight miles away, who can tell?

At the dinner table, I imagine
hovering over the shadowy windshield.
No ski masks, no sage smoking
on the dashboard.
Maybe in the backseat, a shotgun, a 12-gauger.
Someone's on the run
            in Wonder Valley.

3/21/18

## *The Leonardo Mountains*

I was always a child of the city,
I always loved the crowded sidewalks,
the old museums and the refined culture.
In the midst of the noise of the city,
I accepted the silence between the people
around me as the price for
a life of the mind.

But the cost of life
amongst the skyscrapers
and the run-down apartments
was beyond my reach
and now I find myself
before the raw mountains
and the tough, green shrubs,
at a distance from the sidewalks
and the cool faces.

Perhaps I truly find myself
now in the midst
of the mind's silence.

But each time I face
the mountains, angular
and sharp and blue in the distance,
I remember the canvases of Leonardo,
and in my mind,
culture is still alive
and worth the pain
of exile from the distant city.

5/11/15

## The Nest

It's an American solitude.

Photographing yourself in a face mask,
extracting a dove's nest
from the dusty eaves of the patio,
the chilly wind blowing dried bird shit
across the Mexican tiles.

It's an American loneliness.

At the "edge of the frontier,"
where the neighbors keep their distance
and the mountains keep their silence,
you strip down at the door step
and shake the bird shit
out of your jeans and t-shirt.

It's toxic.

An American emptiness.

12/05/17

George Howell

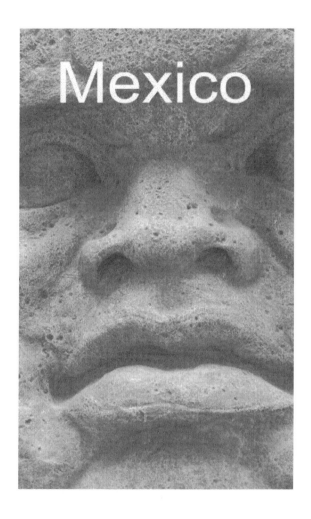

## *Pájaros Callados*
### *Gracias a Alberto Garcia Zatarain*

Tus palabras amargas
me retan cada día.

Por la mañana,
en la cama solitaria,
los rayos del sol vuelan
a lo largo de las paredes
como pájaros de oro,
pájaros sin voz.

No encuentro mis palabras,
las palabras que se escapan
como pájaros callados.

El cuarto brilla con la luz del sol.
La cama espera en la sombra, silencio.

Tus palabras amargas
me retan cada día.

El rayo de sol
se posa en la mano como pájaro,
espera un momento largo
y después, se va.

Las palabras se escapan
como pájaros callados.
En la cama.
En la sombra.
Solo.

3/21/17

## Quiet Birds
*Thanks to Alberto Garcia Zatarain*

Your bitter words
challenge me every day.

In the morning,
in the lonely bed,
the rays of the sun fly
along the walls
like golden birds,
silent birds.

I cannot find my words,
the words that escape
like quiet birds.

The room shines with the light of the sun.
The bed waits in the shade, speechless.

Your bitter words
challenge me every day.

The sunbeam
perches in my hand like a bird,
waits a long moment
and then is gone.

The words escape
like quiet birds.
In the bed.
In the shadow.
Solitary.

3/21/17

## Los Dos Gallos

¡Qué coloroso el gallo jovencito!
Con las plumas amarillas y oros,
las coberteras blancas y moradas,
el pecho hinchado con el poder
de sus seis meses en esta tierra.

"Es demasiado joven para pelear,"
dice el hombre llevando la mascara
de soldador que describe a nos
el cuento de los gallos en cuatro jaulas
que descubrimos mientras que
buscamos garrafón cerámica
por la cocina.

"Estos son gallos de pelea,"
nos dice el hombre
que trabaja en el taller mecánico
al lado del jardín
donde se apilan las jaulas.

"Y quién es el campeón?"
Lo pregunto.

Nos muestra un gallo magro
que aparece como buitre
con la cabeza afeitada
y el cuello torcido.

## The Two Roosters

The young rooster is bursting with color,
with his yellow and gold plumes,
his tail feathers purple and white,
his chest swollen with the power
of his six months on this earth.

"He's too young to fight,"
says the guy wearing a welder's mask
who tells us the story of the roosters
in four cages we discovered
while looking for a ceramic water jug
for our kitchen.

"These are fighting cocks,"
says the young guy
who works in the auto shop
next to the garden
where the cages are stacked.

"And who is the champion?"
I ask him.

He shows us a skinny rooster
who looks like a vulture
with his shaved head
and crooked neck.

"Se cortan la cresta y las barbillas,"
nos dice, "para pelear mejor.
Este ha ganado cuatro veces."

Y entonces,
nos muestra la cicatriz larga y blanca
que corre por la pierna.

"Y después de la última lucha,
es comido el gallo?"

El hombre ríe. "No, es libre
para criar más gallitos
como eso jovencito por allá."
Apunta al envanecido
que no ha aún sido
degradado por el éxito
en la lucha.

7/19/15

"They cut off his crest and wattles
so he can fight better. He's already won
four fights."

And then he shows us the long, white scar
running down its leg.

"And after his last fight—
Do you eat him?"

The guy laughs.
"No, he's free to have more little ones,
like that cocky guy over there."
He points to the puffed up rooster
who hasn't yet been degraded
by success in the ring.

7/19/15

## *Earthquake*

In Tijuana, 1,700 miles
from Mexico City,
Facebook friends puzzle over
the search for an imaginary girl
in the pile of glass & bricks
that once was a school.

Meanwhile, in TJ,
when dead bodies
& police cars block the streets,
they joke about taking detours
to get to the Oxxo.

Fear & anger do close the heart.

Someone writes,
if she is only imaginary,
our hearts won't break
if they don't find her.

Last week, in Puebla,
someone murdered
a drunk girl
who fell asleep in a cab.

All of Mexico shook.

They couldn't rescue her
& they never expected
the buildings to wobble & fall
in Roma or Xochimilco
this week.

On the other side of the border,
at a laptop's distance
from the pain in Mexico,
I wonder –
Is the search for
an imaginary girl
a second chance for themselves
to escape from the crime,
the cynicism & the shifting ground?

9/22/17

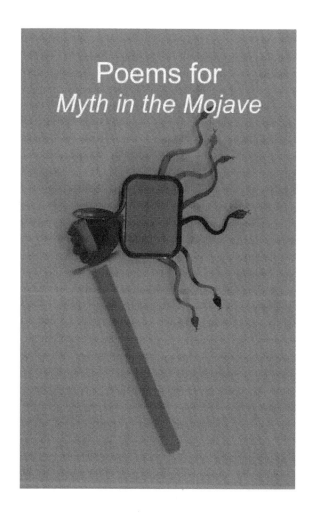

## Wounded

I take things too seriously,
take things to heart,
      a cliché, yes
but the things I laugh at
often come back as a heartache
and an inspiration.

My chalice is tongue-in-cheek.
      Yes, a bucket from Home Depot
      on a table leg and an old cutting board.

Not sure, at first
how much I believed
in the Holy Grail
as myth.

But why can't the sacred lie
in ordinary things?
      The grail a serving plate,
      a goblet,
            utensils for eating and drinking
            sacred for what they do,
            not what they are.

The blood of Christ
caught in a silver cup,
the wounding,
and the gnawing consciousness
of guilt,
      wounded,
            a shame.

Yearning for a place in the spirit,
I took communion
and sang the Old Testament psalms
and ultimately left the Church,
again.

This is the nature of guilt and shame,
the duality of heart and mind—
            I feel deeply
                        what I cannot believe in.

I love the earth,
the mountains and the stars,
the material presence
as illusory as light,
as mercurial
as an intuition.

A materialist
in the house of the spirit,
I take things too seriously.

I trust in the heart
to heal its wounds.

3/13/15

## *The Flower Maidens of Tijuana*

How many times can you
tell this tale?
How many times before
you become the "pure fool,
enlightened by compassion?"

Nietzsche laughed at Parzifal,
called the chastity of Wagner's hero
a perversion of natural desires.

And certainly it is safer, saner
to search for solitude
among the rocks
     and the flower maidens
     of the Mojave –
          Rock Daisy & Desert Lily
          White Layia and the others—
Looking for yourself
in the piles of granite
     stacked like blocks, fissured
     and grainy to the hand
     when you rub your palm across
     the hip or thigh of a boulder.

But when there is no love,
there is always the distraction
of adventure.

Poor fool,
drunk on Tecate
and falling in
with the flower maidens of Tijuana.

Tossing dollars
          on the mostly naked dancer
          sprawled on the dance floor,
          while drunken meseras
                    dry hump guys in stud cuts
                    in shadowy corners
and stumbling
into a deserted bar,
          where a young dancer
          listlessly strips down
                    to nothing but her sneakers.
Later, she sits with her arm
around your shoulder
and you buy more beers
and she pushes you
into the arms
          of a hefty dancer
          who cradles your face
          in her big, soft chest,
          slapping your face
          with her breasts.

The young dancer says
"Come with me to the cabana"
and then moves on to the next table
when you tell her you are broke.

You always felt badly
for the young gal,
            dancing naked for the drunks
            and fucking them for pesos.

In the eighties, in the age of AIDS.
Dangerous.

How many times have you
told this as a "crazy-drunk-in-Mexico" story?

Sober now,
can you tell this tale
with compassion
in your heart
            for yourself
            and for the others?

Perhaps the grail lies hidden
amongst the flower maidens of the Mojave,
            searching for yourself
            in the solitude
            of the mountains
                        and the freshly blooming
                        wildflowers of spring.

Shifting from the safety of the second person
to the openness of the first,
I own my story.

I don't speak for the mountains
and the mountains don't speak for me.

Sober now,
and married,
under the protection
and trust of love,
       I say the grail
       is the heart
       reconciled with its sadness
       and its possibilities,
              telling an old story
              with a new ending.

3/18/15

## *Medusa is not*

Medusa is not my thing.
Medusa is not California,
      though the hot breath of the desert
      turns the skin to dust
      and maybe she wears
      yellow desert wildflowers in her hair
      as the snaky white lines of the highway
      slither into the reflecting pool
      of a mirage and vanish.

And if she were naked?
I wouldn't look.
Medusa is not my thing.

In the mythology of mirrors,
in the tale of what you see
      and what you won't,
you must look in retrospect
at what you cannot face,
      or your heart will turn to stone.

What you don't see
is behind you now
      and waiting in the future
      is the Medusa in the rear-view mirror.

3/15/14

Poems of Loss
& Mourning

## Petals
### For Fiorella Ottolini & Laura Peterson-Volz

Petals, I thought,
or leaves falling
from the tree of life—
Too sentimental
for these farewells,
knowing more petals
and leaves will fall?

In Agrigento,
broken clay figures
on a shelf,
Demeter and Persephone—
Offerings for those
gone underground,
for the figs and olives
and wheat
to come back around.

Not so sentimental—
We all go underground.

A poem grows like a flower
or a little leaf unfurling.

Our friends have passed.
We will follow.

3/28/18

## Queen Madeleine's Retreat
*For Madeleine Schneidman*

Since we were here last,
orange balls, bright as paper lanterns,
hang from
the waxy succulent,
and once we leave,
more leopard spots
will spread along
its rows of swollen branches.

Do you remember my name?

Age has taken so much from you
since the last time
I sat on this sundeck
to read or watch the sparrow hawks
drifting over Brentwood Canyon.

You have lost so much.
More bells will grow.
More spots will spread
once you, too, are gone.

3/17/09

## Yellow Flowers
### For Betty Brown

Yellow flowers on a window sill—
The first thing you see
or the last,
waking and sleeping
in the hospital bed
in your daughter's room?

Do you focus on the tiny cars and trucks
racing back and forth on the 134,
framed within your window,
like toy cars your grandson
might want to snatch and race
across the living room rug?

Opening your eyes or closing them,
drifting off to sleep
in the middle of a word,
a little broth and some tea
to sustain you.

Yellow flowers on a window sill
to distract our attention
from the thin wisps
of hair that refuse to behave.

We don't know you well,
Betty Brown.
We have seen our own mothers
slowly drifting off
to the quiet emptiness
beyond the flowers
sunning in the window frame.

We wish you peace
on the approaching day
when you close your eyes
and the yellow flowers
go away.

5/29/13

## *The Sandals*

I wore the sandals
you gave me,
the tops of my feet
brown from walking
along the beach
with your mother.

We often sat
around the dinner table,
talking about the beach,
but you were absent
and we talked
with circumspect sadness
and anger
and walked along the beach
whenever we could.

I loved the hard
wash of the waves
and the salt buoying
my body in the surf,
a sensual bath of salt
and saw on occasion
the fat shadow of a
sea lion passing under
the water,

and once saw a stingray
shoot past my legs
as the tide pulled
the sand out from
under my feet.

After a long weekend away,
the beach changed.

We followed new
shorebirds passing
through on their fall migrations
and the ocean was warmer
and the big families
abandoned the umbrellas
and colorful canopies,
the kids back in school now.
It was a sad time, really.

A young man
had drowned while
we were gone.
He'd gone too far,
showing off for his girlfriend
and was pulled under
by the rip tide.

We often noted
young men and women
walking past us,
teasing each other,
new to love,
and wondered if
any of these young men
was the one who drowned?

The beach had changed
and we honored the change
by walking patiently,
reflecting on our gains
and losses of this summer.

I never got to tell you
how much I liked
the sandals.
You absented yourself
and we had only ourselves
to talk to.
Which was as it should be.

I'm wearing the sandals now
as I write this.

9/14/15

## Contrails

I noticed that the pepper tree
is gone, a tree of life
we planted over Chuck's ashes,
and the circle where we sat
remembering our old friend
is replaced with a swimming pool.

It'll be 95 today,
and many of us
who sang and cried and wished
our friend a good farewell
will float on our backs
and watch the contrails overhead
dissolve into wispy
nothings.

5/12/12

George Howell

## *Headlights on the Rolling Hills*

A hand once swept across
this darkness, pushing up
    the hills that swallow
    my headlights,
pushed up the hills,
rising and dropping in the night,
    and I speed along,
      scanning for red-eyed coyotes
        scrambling across the road bed.

We meet like this, at night,
your headlights in the rear view mirror,
    the ghost light of your car
    sweeping under my car,
      its shadow imprinted on the hills
      and vanishing when you drop into a dip.

We meet like this as if the hand
that pushed these hills in place
    so many heartbeats ago
    set our wheels in motion.

I don't want to be lonely.

I love the rush of the unknown,
      speeding down these hills at night,
      meant to follow and to lead,
      headlights on a back road.

Over how many hills will time lead me?
And who will puzzle over the hillside shadows
when my headlights go out forever?

Do you, too, think about dying
on a dark road in the desert,
        your headlights shining
        in the rear view mirror,
        my car leading the way?

10/29/16

## *If you find Buddha, shoot him*

In this practice, close your eyes
and imagine blowing out a candle
with your handgun.

Always carry bullets in the glove box,
the right gun will surely find you,
though we can't draw conclusions
from a broken hotel window.

325 million guns in America,
enough for one gun in every hotel room.
Store the excess firearms in the ballroom.

If I hit you, will you kiss me?

Mindfulness is also an essential practice
for snipers on the post-industrial battlefield.

They dropped cluster bombs
on the wedding party.

Resisting the weather, we deny
the reality of our thoughts,
which are cocked and loaded.

The parking lot littered with boots,
cowboy hats, bloody bandanas.

If I kiss you, will you shoot me?

9/27/17

## Cul de Sac

The mountains to the east
are neutral, featureless
in the pre-dawn light.

That is the condition
of this place,
looking through the window,
at this moment,
looking for certainty
and only finding
a cul de sac,
that place that wakes me up
at three in the morning,
words reverberating,
threats, accusations, rage—
The sun not yet
reddening the tips of the mountains.

Close the bedroom door,
it's cold out there.

My brother calls it
PTSD.

The mountains are heartless
and I am alone.

My goal this year:
start the motor
and drive myself out
of the cul de sac.

11/7/16

## *The fire in the chicken coops*

In my childhood memories,
my grandfather's house casts a long shadow.
It still stands near the grove of trees
that swallowed up
his abandoned chicken coops.

You can't trust a child's memories.
I don't trust mine.

Did the chickens run free in the basement?
I think I remember the stink and the noise
in the unfinished cellar
where he cooped up his family
and built a house over their heads.

My father remembered chipping ice off
the basement walls in the heart of winter.

I remember aunts and uncles
sitting around our kitchen table,
drinking beers and squawking,
pushing the shame of unspoken stories
under the table legs
like a stuffed toy
a child could cradle.

My grandfather scared me.

Bald head like a cracked egg,
bandy-legged walk like a fighting cock,
voice as raspy as a chicken scratching gravel,
chin bristly as a coxcomb.

"Come here, little boy!
Let me give you a kiss."

How can a child know
what an adult really wants?

I only found out later he wanted
to make his fortune selling chickens.

Not long ago, my cousin, who slept in the bed
where he was caught
with one of the step-daughters,
took us to the woods,
the coops collapsed like bombed out bunkers,
½ of his chickens lost,
screeching as they burned.

I didn't ask, but I wondered, did he go to jail
before or after the chickens burned?

I can picture the house to this day.
I just don't trust what I remember.

6/7/18

## *68th Birthday*

Posts from New England,
fall trees flaming
          like birthday candles
and feeling nostalgic,
I wrote, "the mountains never change here,
beauty is monotonous."

San Gorgonio on the horizon,
drab and dry,
waiting for the rain and snow,
waiting for the white hump on the horizon
to become a mythical whale.

Where is our place on earth?
In the distant horizon line,
that calls you like ambition and high hopes,
or someplace buried inside the skin,
a dialogue with the shadow
that follows you on your morning walk?

Sixty-eight years on the planet.
Many have come before me,
many more will follow.
A day to reflect
and look for a place
to light a candle
of hope.

11/6/16

## *Keys*
*For Thomas R. Wilson*

I can't get the house key
back on the key chain,
there are just too many keys –
2 car keys,
2 keys for the house in the desert,
1 key for the house in San Diego,
& another key I don't recognize at first.

It opens an empty townhouse
with wood floors that squeak
when someone walks on them,
the blinds drawn,
the living room walls bare & dark.

Six weeks ago.

I have to stop & count back
the weeks,
a short time, really,
to forget why I have
your house key.

Grieving gets to me
in odd ways.

I fit the house key
on the key chain
& a poem opens.

Thank God for keys.

9/6/17

# Notes on the poems

"Martin Mull" describes a 2010 painting exhibit by the actor-comedian and musician.

"The Mountain/Ahab in the Desert" was written for David Landrey's 2015 Moby Dick project held in Buffalo, NY.

"Pájaros Callados" acknowledges translation help from Alberto Garcia Zatarain, a fine poet, musician and friend who lives outside of Rosarito, Baja California Norte.

In "Earthquake," "Oxxo" refers to a "7-11"-like convenience store.

"Medusa is not," "The Flower Maidens of Tijuana" and "Wounded" were written for, and presented at, the Medusa (2014) and The Holy Grail (2015) projects organized by Dr. Catherine Svehla as part of her Myth in Mojave series. Some of these were included in radio presentations following the events, which took place at The Beatnik Lounge, in Joshua Tree, CA.

The section photo for Myth in the Mojave is of an assemblage for the Medusa exhibit. "Wounded" describes my chalice sculpture for The Holy Grail exhibit.

"Petals" refers to the relics of goddess worship found at Agrigento, Sicily, which I saw in 2016.

Where is our place on earth?
In the distant horizon line,
that calls you like ambition and high hopes,
or someplace buried inside the skin,
in a dialogue with the shadow
that follows you on your morning walk?
-68th Birthday

**George Howell**

I live in Wonder Valley, a sparse, spread-out community about eight miles east of Twentynine Palms, California. Maybe due of its isolation, our valley has gained a reputation as a "spiritual" place where you go for solitary reflection, though the house often shakes when the Marines practice for desert warfare in the mountains to the north.

Sometimes I find solitude here, and sometimes I'm guilty of the pathetic fallacy, writing my needs and fears on an indifferent landscape. Sometimes I take things too seriously. I also like to laugh and have fun. I'd like to think my poetry reflects the light from all of these angles.

Recent books published by Cholla Needles:

Susan Abbott – Nasty Woman Rise
Tobi Alfier – Slices of Alice
Cynthia Anderson – Waking Life
Brian Beatty – Dust and Stars
Dave Benson – Stone Soup
Steve Braff – 40 Days
Michael H. Brownstein – A Slipknot Into Somewhere Else
Robert DeLoyd – Upon Ashen Roads
Jean-Paul Garnier – In Iudicio
Greg Gilbert - Afflatus
Lucy Griffith – A Burro And A Broke-In Hat
Katia Aoun Hage – After The War The Women Spoke
Connetta Jean – Picture A Haiku
Kendall Johnson & John Brantingham
  – A Sublime and Tragic Dance
Kendall Johnson – A Whole Lotta Shakin'
Zara Kand – Interiors
Zara Kand – Exteriors
Noreen Lawlor – Sacred Possibilities
Noreen Lawlor – Tangled Limbs And Prayers
Dave Maresh – A Book That Turned Up One Day
Dave Maresh – Garage Band
James Marvelle – Lasting Notes
James Marvelle – Walking In The Light
Rees Nielsen – That's What I Painted
Cindy Rinne & Nikia Chaney - Mapless
Cindy Rinne – Moon of Many Petals
Ram Krishna Singh – God Too Awaits Light
John Sierpinski – Sucker Hole
Michael Dwayne Smith – Roadside Epiphanies
r soos – during the music

Come enjoy our monthly readings at Space Cowboy Books.
Thank you for reading!     https://www.chollaneedles.com

All Cholla Needles Books are available on Amazon.com

Made in the USA
Middletown, DE
24 March 2019